Marguerite Patten

Junior Cook Book

Illustrations by Eileen Strange

A Piccolo Book
Pan Books Ltd, London

This book has been compiled from *Adventures in Cookery*
(Books 1 and 2) first published 1967 by Ginn and
Company Ltd.
First published in this form 1971 by Pan Books Ltd,
33 Tothill Street, London, S.W.1.

ISBN 0 330 02823 5

Printed in Great Britain by
Cox & Wyman Ltd, London, Reading and Fakenham

CONTENTS

vi

INTRODUCTION

COOKING IS FUN and once you have mastered the easy dishes in this book, you will have made a flying start towards becoming a good cook. It is very satisfying to serve your family or friends with a tasty meal or snack that you have made all yourself.

Here are the sorts of recipe you will find in this book:

> GETTING BREAKFAST
> MAKING DRINKS
> MAKING SANDWICHES
> MAKING QUICK SNACKS
> MAKING SALADS
> MAKING PUDDINGS
> TEA TIME
> PARTIES AND PICNICS

Each recipe in the book tells you exactly how many servings it will make. If you want to make more or less, you simply halve or double the quantities.

Before you start cooking I think it would help if you read pages ix–xiii for they explain about some of the 'tools' you will use for cooking and some of the words you will find in the recipes. May I remind you about two important things: *Please do be careful* when you use knives and hot cookers;

see saucepan handles are turned in towards the cooker; if you do burn your fingers on hot tins, etc, immediately cool them in cold water and let a grown-up know. *Do clear up as you work*, it makes it easier for you and grown-ups will be more likely to let you do some cooking again if there is no mess.

Good luck and I hope you like the book.

Marguerite Patten

SOME TOOLS YOU WILL USE

Here are some of the tools mentioned in recipes:

Frying-pans and saucepans: make sure you choose them large enough for the amount of food. If you have non-stick pans ask a grown-up how to take care of them.

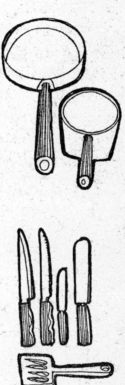

Knives: are very important when you cook. ALWAYS BE VERY CAREFUL HOW YOU USE A SHARP KNIFE which you need for cutting and chopping. Always ask a grown-up to help you chop difficult things. If you have a chopping board, cut on this, so you do not mark the table. Cut bread with a bread knife on a bread or chopping board unless you are using ready sliced bread. Spread butter on bread with a flat-bladed knife; a pointed knife makes holes in the bread. Lift food out of pans, etc, with a wide-bladed knife called a palette knife, or use a fish slice, that looks like this.

Spoons: when you stir use a wooden spoon; but when you measure use the type of spoon in the recipe.

ALWAYS HAVE JUST ENOUGH
FOOD TO GIVE A LEVEL SPOON
MEASURE. IF YOU OVER-FILL
THE SPOON YOU HAVE TOO
MUCH FOR THE RECIPE.

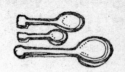

Scales: If you have no scales a grown-up
will help you work out the amounts.
Today some people use Metric measures
(grammes and kilos), others use
Imperial measures (ounces and pounds).
This book gives you both; Metric
measures come first and Imperial follow
in brackets immediately afterwards, so
you can choose which to follow.

Measures: if you have a proper measure
use this, but a *teacup holds about 142ml*
($\frac{1}{4}$ *pint*); a breakfast cup about 284 ml
($\frac{1}{2}$ pint). Many recipes give spoon
measures. Always fill the spoon so that
it is *level* NOT more.

A grater: is used for making pieces of
cheese, lemon rind, etc, smaller and if
you rub a slice of bread against the
coarse side of the grater you make
breadcrumbs. The picture shows the
most usual kind.

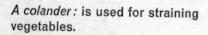

A colander: is used for straining
vegetables.

Sieves: for straining liquids. Use small
ones for tea, etc, larger ones where there
is more liquid. You also need a sieve to
make sure there are no lumps in flour.

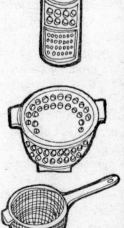

A pastry brush: is used for many things including greasing tins and dishes. Take a very little margarine or fat from the amount in the recipe, warm this and brush over the dish, or rub the unmelted fat over the tin or dish with greaseproof paper.

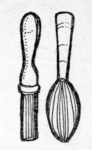

An egg whisk or *rotary whisk:* is used to whip cream, beat up egg white, etc.

Cake tins: there are many sorts of cake tins, but for the recipes in this book you will need a baking tray, patty tins, paper cake cases, and a sandwich tin.

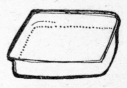

Basins and bowls: you will need a nice big mixing bowl (never try to mix a recipe in too small a bowl, it is very difficult!) and some smaller basins for whisking egg, whipping cream, and so on.

WORDS USED IN COOKING

Mixing

BEATING: means mixing the ingredients together with a very brisk movement. A wooden spoon is generally used.

BLENDING: also means mixing the ingredients together.

CREAMING: means beating fat and sugar together until they are soft and fluffy; use a wooden spoon.

FOLDING: is a turning movement done gently and slowly with a metal spoon, as in the Fruit Snow (pages 88–89)

KNEADING: means mixing the ingredients firmly together with your hands, as in the Vanilla Biscuits (pages 131–2)

RUBBING IN: is a method of mixing fat with flour with the tips of your fingers; you do this in the Fruit Crumble (pages 101–2) and in Scones and Rock Buns (pages 113–17 and 118–20).

WHISKING: is a very brisk movement to whip cream or egg whites and is done by hand or with a rotary whisk.

Cooking

BAKING: is the method of cooking food in the oven, such as cakes.

BOILING: is cooking in liquid at boiling point (100°C or 212°F), eg, as you boil the cauliflower as on page 69.

FRYING: is cooking in fat; do be careful when you do this, see page 8 which tells you about testing the temperature of the fat.

GRILLING: is cooking under the grill in a quick heat.

SIMMERING: is steady cooking in liquid. You should see an occasional bubble on the surface.

WARMING: hot foods should be served on hot plates or dishes. Heat these on racks on the top of the cooker, in the warming compartment or in the oven set very low.

SYMBOLS USED IN THIS BOOK

This means you will need to light the gas oven or switch on the electric oven. Your mother may prefer to do this for you. If you have a solid-fuel oven ask your mother or a grown-up to explain this.

This symbol is for the grill, and shows that you will need to use it.

This shows that you use the top of the cooker. Ask your mother to explain how to turn down the burner or hotplate during cooking.

This means you need to weigh the food on scales. This book gives both Metric weights (grammes and kilos) and Imperial weights (oz and lb).

MAKING
BREAKFAST

MAKING BREAKFAST

It would be a very nice surprise for the family if you prepared breakfast one morning. Here are three breakfast menus you might try, depending on what sort of breakfast your family likes:

Menu 1
Cornflakes or other breakfast cereal with milk and sugar.
Toast or bread, butter, and marmalade or honey.
Coffee (with cold or hot milk and sugar) (pages 23–4).

Menu 2
Orange juice.
Boiled eggs (pages 9–10).
Toast, butter, marmalade.
Tea (you will need cold milk and sugar on the table) (pages 21–2).

Menu 3
Halved fresh grapefruit or canned grapefruit. Bacon and egg (pages 11–13).
Toast, butter, marmalade.
Tea (you will need cold milk and sugar on the table) (pages 21–2).

Step by Step to Breakfast

A. Decide on your menu.

B. Lay the table.

C. *If you decide on Menu 1*

1 Put on the water for the coffee.

2 Put the cereal, etc, on the table.

3 Toast the bread (see below).
Put it on the table with butter and
marmalade or honey.

4 Make the coffee and heat the milk.

How to make toast when you have no
electric toaster

1 Light the gas grill or switch on the
electric grill.

2 Let the grill heat for 1–2 minutes so
that the toast browns quickly without
becoming too hard. You can be slicing
the bread while you are waiting.

3 Put the slices of bread on the grid of
the grill pan.

4 Watch it as it browns on one side.

5 Turn it over and let it brown on the
other side.

3

6 When the toast is ready, stand it up so that it does not become limp but stays crisp. This is best done in a toast rack.

D. *If you decide on Menu 2*

1 Halve and squeeze out the oranges. Pour into small glasses.

2 Toast the bread (see above) and put in a rack on the table with the butter and marmalade.

3 Put on the water for cooking the eggs.

4 Put on the water for making the tea and put the milk and sugar on the table.

5 Make the tea, carry this carefully to the table.

6 Put in the eggs and time (see page 10).

E. *If you decide on Menu 3*

1 Either cut the grapefruit in halves and separate the pieces of fruit with the tip of a sharp knife, put sugar on the table, *or* open a can of grapefruit and spoon the segments (pieces) and some juice into bowls or grapefruit glasses.

2 Put the plates for bacon and eggs to warm in a low oven, add 1 extra plate.

3 Toast the bread (see pages 3–4) and put in a rack on the table with the butter and marmalade.

4 Cook the bacon in a frying-pan or under the grill and keep warm on the extra plate (see page 12).

5 Put on the kettle for tea.

6 Make the tea and carry this carefully to the table, put the milk on the table also.

7 Fry the eggs (see pages 11–12) and lift on to the plates with the bacon; keep warm until you have eaten the grapefruit.

Making overnight preparations

If you are in a hurry in the morning, it is a good idea to do some jobs for breakfast the night before.

1 You can lay the table, and put everything ready for making tea or coffee, except the milk which should be kept in a cool place.

2 You can prepare the grapefruit or orange juice.

Laying the table for breakfast

1 Put a tablecloth or mats on the table, add serviettes.

2 If you have bacon, or other hot food, you need large knives and forks. If the table is of polished wood, you will need mats to stop the hot plates marking the surface.

3 Lay small plates and knives for toast.

4 Add cups, saucers and teaspoons, sugar, a jug of cold milk (unless you are heating the milk).

5 Put marmalade and a spoon; butter, with a knife, on the table.

6 Add toast or sliced bread.

7 For grapefruit you need dishes on plates together with spoons, or for fruit juice you need glasses.

8 For boiled eggs you need eggcups on plates and small spoons with salt and pepper.

9 Put a heat-resistant mat or stand for the tea or for coffee *and* hot milk.

WHEN MAKING BREAKFAST

There are many other dishes in this book you can prepare for breakfast – for example, many people like scrambled eggs (pages 56–7), or grilled bacon (pages 62–63), or bacon and sausage (pages 62–3). If you ever visit Norway you may be offered cheese for breakfast. You might try this as a change from eggs and bacon. Poached haddock (page 59) is ideal for breakfast, and cold ham with sliced tomatoes is also good.

When frying bread and eggs you are told to have the fat hot; so watch the fat carefully as it melts. When it has melted put a tiny cube of bread in the pan and if it turns golden brown *in about 1 minute* you can cook the slice of bread and eggs. If it burns or browns more quickly allow the fat to *cool* slightly and test again.

When heating milk for coffee or cereals see it does not boil, but have a large metal spoon all ready. If the milk looks like boiling, *stir briskly* to lower the temperature.

8

How to boil an egg

You will need:

1 egg and water to cover.

You will use:

saucepan, basin, tablespoon, eggcup.

1 Light the gas burner or switch on the hotplate.

2 Take a rather small saucepan; you may have a special egg saucepan.

3 Put in enough cold water to cover the egg (or eggs). This generally means that the saucepan is half-filled.

4 Put the saucepan on the cooker to boil, but do not let the water boil away.

5 Take the egg in a basin so that it does not fall and a tablespoon over to the cooker. Remember that eggs taken straight from the refrigerator or a cold place, tend to crack when you put them in the saucepan.

6 Put the egg into the spoon, and lower it very gently into the water.

7 Immediately, look at the clock, your watch, or the timer on the cooker (which the instruction card or book will tell you how to set).

8 Some people like to put eggs into cold water, bring to the boil and time from this point. Because the egg starts to cook as the water comes to the boil, the cooking time is shorter.

	Really soft-boiled egg	Firm set egg	Hard-boiled egg
If put in cold water	3 mins	4 mins	10 mins
If put in boiling water	4 mins	5 mins	10 mins

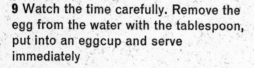

9 Watch the time carefully. Remove the egg from the water with the tablespoon, put into an eggcup and serve immediately

Fried bacon and egg

This is one of the nicest breakfast or supper dishes. Read page 8 about frying first.

You will need:

bacon	1 or 2 rashers
egg	1
fat	15 grammes ($\frac{1}{2}$ oz)

These ingredients will make 1 serving.

You will use:

sharp knife or kitchen scissors, plate for bacon, frying-pan, fork or tongs, saucer or cup, fish slice, serving plate.

1 Light the gas burner or switch on the electric hotplate.

2 Cut the rinds off the bacon (see note at end of recipe). This makes bacon fat crisp better.

3 If the rashers are very long, cut into halves to fit into the frying-pan.

4 Put the bacon rinds into the frying-pan with the bacon, as they give extra fat for cooking the egg.

5 Cook the bacon until the fat is golden in colour, turning once if the bacon is thick. This usually takes about 3 minutes, but varies with the thickness of the rasher.

6 Lift the bacon on to a warmed plate with a fork or tongs, and remove the rinds from the frying-pan. Keep the bacon hot on the serving plate.

7 Crack the eggshell sharply with a knife or against the edge of a saucer or cup.

8 Pull the halves of the shell apart so that the egg gently drops into the saucer or cup.

9 Put fat into the frying-pan and heat until melted.

10 Pour the egg into the hot fat. If you are cooking several eggs in the same pan, put in one egg and turn the heat down when the white starts to set. Put in the second egg, and so on.

11 Cook the egg 2 minutes for a lightly set egg or 3 minutes for a firmer egg.

12 Bring the plate with the bacon near the frying-pan.

13 Lift the egg out of the pan with a fish slice and arrange next to the bacon. Serve as soon as possible.

Cleaning a frying-pan

A greasy frying pan is not very pleasant to wash up so wipe out the pan with newspaper or kitchen paper before washing this. Remember to ask your mother or a grown-up how to clean a non-stick frying pan.

2 ways to cut the rind from bacon:

1 Lay the rasher of bacon on the chopping board and cut away the rind with a sharp knife.

2 Use a pair of kitchen scissors and cut the rind away with these.

Remember to fry rinds to give you extra fat.

Birds love crisp bacon rinds.

Bacon and tomato

Another food that goes well with bacon is a tomato.

You will need:

bacon	1–2 rashers
tomato	1
salt	pinch
pepper	shake

These ingredients will make 1 serving.

You will use:

kitchen scissors, sharp knife, chopping board, frying-pan, tongs, plate.

1 Cut the rinds off the bacon (see picture, page 13) and cut the tomato in half.

2 Sprinkle the cut sides of tomato with a pinch of salt and a shake of pepper.

3 Put the bacon and bacon rinds, which give extra fat, into the pan. Cook 2 minutes for thin rashers; thicker ones will take longer. The picture shows how you arrange the lean of the second rasher over the fat of the first rasher.

4 When the bacon is nearly cooked, put in the tomato halves and cook for 1

minute. Do not overcook, otherwise
tomatoes lose flavour and texture.

5 Lift the bacon and tomato halves on to
the hot plate and serve at once.

Two or three *mushrooms* can be fried
with bacon instead of the tomato.
MAKE SURE they are real mushrooms
if you have picked them – ask a grown-up
to look at them.

1 Wash the mushrooms well, cut the
ends off the stalks. If the mushrooms are
very good there is no need to skin them.

2 Add a small piece of fat to the frying-pan
at stage 3.

3 Then melt this, put in the mushrooms
and cook gently for about 5 minutes.

Bacon and fried bread

Crisp fried bread makes a breakfast or supper more satisfying. Make sure the fat is really hot at stage 2 so the bread browns well.

You will need:

bacon	1–2 rashers
bread	small slice

These ingredients will make 1 serving.

You will use:

sharp knife or kitchen scissors, frying-pan, fork or tongs, plate, bread knife and board, fish slice.

1 Cook the bacon and bacon rinds as fried bacon and egg to stage 4.

2 Lift the bacon onto a hot plate.

3 Make sure the fat in the pan is really hot. Put the slice of bread into the frying-pan and cook for 1 minute. Then turn and cook for another minute until crisp and brown.

Breakfast in bed

You may like to give your mother or father breakfast in bed for a special treat, perhaps on their birthdays, or you may have someone at home who is ill and needs breakfast in bed. You can serve the same kind of menus as on page 2 but remember you have to carry the tray so do not make it too heavy or try to prepare anything too complicated.

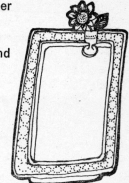

1 Put on a cloth to make the tray look pretty, add a serviette and plate, cup, etc.

2 If it is a special day, like a birthday, perhaps you could put a small flower into a tiny vase or eggcup.

3 Make the toast and put it on the tray, either in a small rack or on a plate, with tiny dishes of butter and marmalade.

4 Prepare orange juice or grapefruit or cereal.

5 Make the tea or coffee. Pour out a cup of tea or coffee, add milk, put on the tray with sugar if wished. *DO NOT try to carry up a tea, or coffee, pot.*

6 Have a final check that everything is on the tray and carry it slowly and carefully to the bedroom.

7 Once you have left the person in bed comfortably eating their breakfast, don't forget to return after five or ten minutes to refill their cup and offer some more toast.

MAKING DRINKS

MAKING DRINKS

In this section you will find tea, coffee, milk shakes and other interesting drinks. Most recipes mention 'cups' – these are teacups.

Remember:
If you are boiling water in a kettle, make sure the lid is firm so it cannot fall off as you pour out the boiling water. Do not fill the kettle more than ¾-full.

Hold the kettle firmly. Pour carefully, with spout away from you, so the steam cannot scald you.

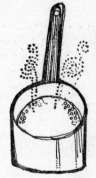

Do not allow milk to *boil* for this gives a skin, just heat the milk until it bubbles round the edge – this is called SIMMERING.
Other recipes talk about SIMMERING when the liquid only bubbles gently.

Fill a 'milky' saucepan with cold water after using it, this makes it easier to wash-up.

When you fill a glass tumbler with a hot drink, pour slowly and keep a spoon *in* the glass. This helps to prevent it cracking.

20

How to make tea

The most important thing to remember is to take the teapot to the kettle, and not the kettle to the teapot. In this way you will be sure of pouring really boiling water on to the tea in the pot.

You will need:

tea, water, milk, sugar.

You will use:

kettle, teapot, spoon, jug, cups and saucers.

1 Put water drawn from the *COLD* tap into the kettle and put it on to heat.

2 Heat teapot with a little hot water from the kettle.

3 Just before the water in the kettle is boiling, pour the water out of the teapot and put in the tea.

4 For one person only, put in 2 *level* teaspoons of tea.

5 We generally say '1 level teaspoon per person and 1 for the pot', so for four people put in 5 *level* teaspoons of tea for a really strong brew. For a weak tea use a little less.

6 The moment the water in the kettle boils, turn or switch off the heat. With an electric kettle, pull out the plug after switching off the heat.

7 Hold the kettle firmly; then pour the boiling water steadily over the tea.

8 Put the lid on the teapot, let it stand for several minutes. Some people stir the tea, *then* let it stand.

9 Pour the cold milk into the jug, then pour a little cold milk into each cup from the jug; everyone helps themselves to sugar if they like it.

10 When the leaves fall to the bottom of the pot the tea is ready to be poured. You can use a tea strainer if you wish.

How to make coffee

There are a number of ways to make coffee. You may have a percolator or other coffee-maker at home, but making it in a jug is a good, as well as easy, way.

You will need:

ground coffee, water, milk, sugar.

You will use:

kettle, tablespoon, jug, coffee strainer, saucepan, cups and saucers.

1 Put water, drawn from the cold water tap, on to boil.

2 *For 1 cup of coffee*: allow $\frac{1}{8}$ litre (142 ml) or $\frac{1}{4}$ pint water, so work out how much water to heat according to the number of cups of coffee you want. For example, for 4 cups of coffee you will need 1 pint or $\frac{1}{2}$ litre of water.

3 Allow about $\frac{1}{2}$ teacup of milk for each person.

4 To $\frac{1}{2}$ litre (568 ml) or 1 pint water use 2 rounded tablespoons (or 4 level tablespoons) of ground coffee.

5 Warm the jug for coffee (as for tea, see page 21). Put in the coffee.

23

6 Pour on the boiling water and let it stand for 1 minute; then stir with a spoon.

7 Put a lid on the coffee jug or use a folded teacloth. Let the coffee stand for 5 minutes in a warm place.

8 Meanwhile heat the milk, do not let it boil for this *spoils* the flavour of coffee and the milk forms a skin which most people dislike. Some people prefer cold milk in coffee.

9 When the coffee is ready, pour it, through a strainer if you have one, into cups or into a warm coffee pot.

10 If you have no strainer, pour carefully for although most of the coffee grounds sink to the bottom, some may rise if you pour too rapidly.

11 Add hot milk to each cup, or pour it into a separate jug and serve immediately.

Drinks with milk

Milk gives lots of interesting drinks for children and grown-ups. The recipes on the next pages show how to make milky drinks of all kinds.

And of course milk is very nice served hot or cold without any flavourings at all.

At bedtime it is a good idea to flavour hot or cold milk with Horlicks or Ovaltine or one of the other malt flavourings.

Read the instructions on the tin and follow these carefully.

You will need to measure the milk in a measuring jug or a cup or a glass you are going to use before making the drinks so no milk is wasted.

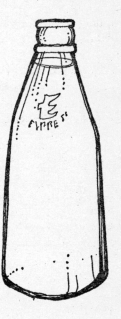

Hot Chocolate

You will need:

milk	1 cup
chocolate powder	2–3 teaspoons

These ingredients will make 1 cup.

You will use:

cup and saucer, saucepan, teaspoon.

1 Heat the milk in a saucepan.

2 Stir in chocolate and pour into a cup. Hot chocolate whisked with a fork or a whisk before it is poured into the cup is frothy and more delicious.

Cocoa

You will need:

*milk (or use half
milk and half water)*   1 cup
cocoa   1 teaspoon
sugar   to taste

These ingredients will make 1 cup.

You will use:

cup and saucer, teaspoon, tablespoon,
saucepan.

1 Put the cocoa into a cup, stir in 2
tablespoons of cold milk, blend until
smooth.

2 Heat the rest of the milk, pour over the
cocoa; add sugar.

Some people like to pour the cocoa
mixture back into the pan and heat it for
1 minute, then return it to the cup.

27

Chocolate Milk Shake

You will need:

milk	1 glass
chocolate powder	2 teaspoons

These ingredients will make 1 glass.

You will use:

teaspoon, bowl, egg whisk, glass.

1 Measure a glassful of milk into the bowl.

2 Whisk in the chocolate powder until it is fully dissolved and the milk looks fluffy.

3 Pour into a clean glass.

You can serve with straws, and add a spoonful of ice-cream for special occasions, or cream and grated chocolate. Chocolate powder is sweetened so no sugar is needed.

Rose hip milk shake

This is a milk shake that gives you the
Vitamin C from rose hip syrup as well as
the food value of milk. The milk should
be really cold.

You will need:

milk	¾ glass
rose hip syrup	1 or 2 tablespoons

These ingredients will make 1 glass.

You will use:

basin, tablespoon, egg whisk, glass.

1 Pour the milk into a basin.

2 Add the rose hip syrup.

3 Whisk together with an egg whisk and
pour into the glass.

More milk shakes

The chocolate and rose hip syrup milk shakes show you how to make a milk shake in a basin. There are many ways of flavouring milk.

1 Whisk the cold milk with a tablespoon of flavoured ice-cream.

2 Use a special sweetened syrup and whisk a tablespoon of this with the cold milk.

3 Use blackcurrant syrup instead of rose hip syrup.

4 You can use a little mashed fresh fruit with the cold milk; whisk a small mashed banana with a teaspoon of sugar and $\frac{3}{4}$ of a glass of cold milk.

5 Whisk 2 tablespoons mashed fresh raspberries and a little sugar with $\frac{3}{4}$ of a glass of cold milk.

To get a very fluffy milk shake, as served in a milk bar, put the ingredients into a fairly tall jug and whisk hard with a flat or rotary beater. If you can use an electric liquidizer or blender belonging to an electric mixer, you will get an even better result.

Quick lemonade

This is very easy to make. Hot lemonade is very good if you have a cold. Be careful the water is not too hot as it will crack the glass, so stand a spoon in the glass (see page 20). You can sweeten with honey instead of sugar.

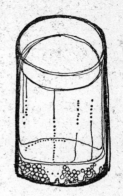

You will need:

lemon	1
sugar	2 teaspoons
water	to taste

These ingredients will make 1 glass.

You will use:

knife, lemon squeezer, teaspoon, glass.

1 Cut the lemon in halves and squeeze out the juice.

2 Put the juice with the sugar into a glass and add hot or cold water.

Economical lemonade

You use the flavour from the lemon peel as well as from the juice.

You will need:

lemons	2 large
sugar	1–2 tablespoons
boiling water	$\frac{5}{8}$ litre (710 ml) or 1$\frac{1}{4}$ pints

These ingredients will make 4 glasses.

You will use:

knife, lemon squeezer, 3 jugs (make sure one of these is safe for boiling water), kettle, tablespoon, strainer.

1 Halve the lemons and squeeze out the juice, put into the smallest jug.

2 Put the lemon halves into a large jug; which has previously been warmed; add sugar. Pour over the boiling water.

3 Let this water cool and, as it cools, press the lemon halves hard to get out as much flavour as possible.

4 Strain into the clean jug and add the lemon juice.

Fruit cup

A special drink for a party.

You will need:

lemons	2
oranges	2
water	1 cup
sugar	50 grammes (2oz)
pineapple juice	1 can
ice cubes	few
soda water	½ litre (568 ml) or 1 pint

to decorate:

orange	1
apple	1
glacé cherries	few

These ingredients will make 8–10 glasses.

You will use:

potato peeler or sharp knife, cup, saucepan, strainer, basin, wooden spoon, lemon squeezer, can opener, large bowl for serving.

1 Cut away the peel from the fruit used in the drink *NOT* in the decoration, and put this in the saucepan and simmer with the water for 5 minutes. (It is very easy to peel fruit with a potato peeler, if you have one.)

33

2 Strain the hot liquid over the sugar which is in a basin.

3 Stir until the sugar has dissolved, then cool.

4 Squeeze the juice from the lemons and oranges, open the can of pineapple juice.

5 Put some ice cubes into the serving bowl, add the fruit juices and the sugar mixture.

6 Just before serving, add the soda water and decorate with the thinly sliced fruit and cherries.

More fruit cups

Now you have made one kind of fruit cup, try others.

Apple fruit cup. Use apple juice instead of pineapple.

Cider cup. Use sweet cider instead of pineapple juice. You can buy non-alcoholic cider as well as the alcoholic kind.

Ginger fruit cup. Use ginger ale or ginger beer; omit soda water.

MAKING
SANDWICHES

MAKING SANDWICHES

When you make sandwiches:

1 Spread the thinly cut slices of bread with butter or margarine and add the filling to half the slices of bread. If you intend to make very dainty sandwiches and cut the crusts off the bread, do not take the filling to the very edges.

2 Cover with the other slices of bread and butter.

3 Put the sandwich on to a chopping board or bread board, remove the crusts if you wish.

4 Cut the whole sandwich into 2 or 4 triangles or squares.

You may like to cut the sandwiches into fingers.

On the next page are some suggestions for SANDWICH FILLINGS, but you will be able to think up many others.

Some sandwich fillings

Cheese. Either put slices of cheese or grated cheese on the bread and butter, or spread cream cheese over the bread and butter; add lettuce or sliced tomato or a little chutney, if wished.

Eggs. You can either hard-boil the eggs and slice them with a knife or egg slicer, or you can make an egg into a more interesting filling (see next page). Lettuce or sprigs of watercress or mustard and cress go well with egg.

Ham. Use thin slices of cooked ham. You can add lettuce or sliced tomato.

Sardine. Open a can of sardines (if you find this difficult, ask a grown-up to help you), put the fish into a basin and mash, adding a pinch of salt and a shake of pepper.

Tomatoes. Slice the tomatoes, put them on bread and butter, add a pinch of salt and a shake of pepper. Add lettuce or sliced cucumber if wished. Some people like a drop of vinegar in tomato sandwiches.

Bananas and Honey. For a delicious, sweet sandwich, spread bread and butter with honey, and add some slices of banana.

39

Egg sandwiches

You will need:

thin slices of bread	2 large or 4 small
butter or margarine	25 grammes (1oz)

for the filling:

eggs	2
butter or margarine	25 grammes (1oz)
salt	pinch
pepper	shake

These ingredients will make 2 servings.

You will use:

saucepan, tablespoon, basin, sharp knife, fork, saucer or plate for butter, bread knife, bread board, flat-bladed knife, plate.

1 Hard-boil the eggs for the time given in the table (see page 10).

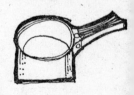

2 As soon as they are cooked, lift out of the water and tap the shells. (This lets the steam out and prevents an ugly dark ring forming round the yolk.)

3 Put into a basin of cold water. Allow the eggs to get quite cold.

4 Remove the shells, put the eggs into a basin and cut them into small pieces with the knife and fork.

40

5 Add the butter or margarine, a pinch of salt and a shake of pepper.

6 Mash everything together with a fork. The mixture is then ready to spread on bread or bread and butter.

7 Spread the bread with the butter.

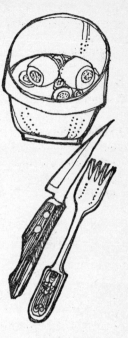

8 Spread half the slices of bread with the egg mixture, then cover with the other slices of bread and butter.

9 Cut away the crusts if wished, then cut the sandwiches into fingers or triangles.

You can spread the bread with potted meat or fish paste at stage 7, then add the egg mixture.

Open sandwiches

In Scandinavia – Denmark, in
particular – open sandwiches are very
popular. The filling is not covered with
a second slice of bread, but lies open on
one slice of bread. Choose any kind of
bread: white, brown, wholemeal or rye
bread or crispbread. Spread the bread
with plenty of butter, and arrange the
food on top. Here are some ideas for
fillings:

1 Roll up thin slices of cooked ham or
luncheon meat, arrange on the buttered
bread, and top with a little mayonnaise
or cream cheese and parsley or slice of
orange.

2 Put a lettuce leaf on the buttered bread,
then add sliced cheese and halved
grapes; take out the grape pips before
putting on to the cheese.

3 Put a lettuce leaf on the buttered
bread, then add slices of hard-boiled egg
and sliced tomato.

Open sandwiches make a good snack if
you have a few friends visiting you.

Toasted cheese club sandwich

You will need:

white or brown bread	3 slices
thinly sliced Cheddar cheese	25–50 grammes (1–2 oz)
made mustard	a little
thinly sliced tomato	1
grilled bacon	1–2 rashers
lettuce leaf	1
salad cream or mayonnaise	a little

These ingredients will make 1–2 servings.

You will use:

plate, sharp knife, chopping board, flat-bladed knife, teaspoon.

1 Switch on or light the grill.

2 Toast the bread on both sides; grill the bacon.

3 Cover one slice with the cheese and a little mustard, and the thinly sliced tomato.

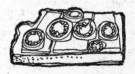

4 Lay the second slice of toast on top, and then the grilled bacon.

5 Top with a lettuce leaf and a little salad cream or mayonnaise and the third slice of toast.

43

6 Cut across, and serve at once.

There are many varieties of toasted
sandwiches, for example:
(*a*) Sliced ham and sliced cheese.
(*b*) Mashed sardines and chopped hard-
boiled egg.
(*c*) Flaked canned salmon and chopped
gherkin.
(*d*) Fried bacon and fried egg.

Preparations to make ahead:
Cut the rind off the bacon with kitchen
scissors or a knife.
Slice the bread, unless using sliced
bread, the cheese and tomato.
Wash the lettuce (see page 78).

MAKING QUICK
SNACKS

MAKING QUICK SNACKS

There are many kinds of quick and easy snacks, and you can serve these for supper or for tea.

I hope you enjoy the recipes here. They show you how to make snacks that are served on toast and others that are rather more substantial.

If you plan to serve the snacks on trays – lay the trays *before* you start cooking the food; cut toasted snacks into fingers so they are easier to manage.

If you prefer to eat them sitting at the table – then the section on pages 111 and 112 will help you lay the table so you do not forget anything.

When making snacks remember:

1 Put the plates to warm first, in a warming drawer or very low oven.

2 Do not try and do too many things at one time; for example, when making a toasted snack watch the toast and then do the topping. You can put the buttered toast on the warm plates until you are ready to add the other ingredients.

3 Serve the snacks as soon as they are made.

Cheese on toast

You will need:

bread	1 slice
butter or margarine	15 grammes ($\frac{1}{2}$ oz)
Cheddar or	
processed cheese	1 slice

These ingredients will make 1 serving.

You will use:

bread knife, bread board, flat-bladed knife, knife for cutting cheese, serving plate.

1 Light the gas grill or switch on the electric grill.

2 Toast the bread on both sides and spread with butter on one side, then cover the buttered side with cheese; put under the hot grill until the cheese begins to melt and bubble. This takes 2–3 minutes.

3 DO NOT OVERCOOK otherwise the cheese becomes TOUGH. The crusts can be cut from the bread, but if left on you have a more substantial meal.

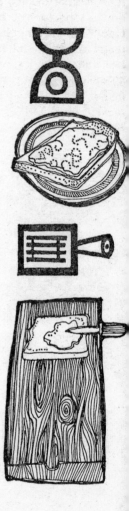

Welsh rarebit

You will need:

butter	15 grammes ($\frac{1}{2}$ oz)
grated cheese	50 grammes (2 oz)
made mustard	$\frac{1}{4}$ level teaspoon
salt	pinch
pepper	shake
milk	$\frac{1}{2}$ tablespoon
bread for toast	1 slice

to garnish:
parsley or	
watercress	sprig

These ingredients will make 1 serving.

You will use:

basin, wooden spoon, grater, plate,
teaspoon, tablespoon, bread knife,
bread board, flat-bladed knife,
serving plate.

1 Switch on or light the grill.

2 Put the butter into a basin, cream
until soft with a wooden spoon, then add
rest of ingredients (except the parsley or
watercress) and stir thoroughly.

3 Toast the bread, remove the crusts if
you wish, spread with the rarebit mixture.

49

4 Put on to the grill pan and cook under the grill for 3–4 minutes, until brown.

Serve at once, garnished with parsley or watercress.

Now you have made a Welsh Rarebit you may like to make more exciting cheese snacks.

Tomato Welsh rarebit

You will need:

Ingredients as Welsh Rarebit plus 1 tomato.

Make the cheese mixture as above.

Toast and butter the bread.

Slice the tomato, then put on the toast, cover with the cheese mixture.

Cook as before.

Yorkshire rarebit

You will need:

Ingredients as Welsh Rarebit plus 1
slice of ham.

1 Make the cheese mixture as before.

2 Toast the bread, butter it, then top
with the ham slice.

3 Cover with the rarebit mixture
and cook as before.

Sardine rarebit

You will need:

ngredients as Welsh Rarebit plus 2
ardines.

Make the cheese mixture as before,
nd the toast.

Cook the rarebit mixture until brown,
op with the sardines and heat for 1
ninute only.

Cut into 2 fingers – see picture.

Beans on toast

This is very easy and well known, and it makes a tasty snack and is a good protein food.

You will need:

beans in tomato sauce	1 small can
bread	1 slice
butter or margarine	15 grammes ($\frac{1}{2}$ oz)

These ingredients will make 1 or 2 small servings.

You will use:

can opener, saucepan, bread knife, bread board, flat-bladed knife, plate.

1 Light the gas grill or switch on the electric grill.

2 Heat beans as directed on can. DO NOT OVERCOOK, as the beans will break and become mushy. The flavour is improved if you add a knob of butter and a *little* pepper to the beans as they cook.

3 Toast bread on both sides; spread with butter on one side.

Put toast on the plate and pile the hot beans on top. Soak the saucepan in cold water immediately.

To make beans on toast more exciting, you can serve with a rasher of grilled bacon and a tomato halved and grilled.

Scrambled egg

You will need:

bread	1 slice
butter or margarine	15 grammes ($\frac{1}{2}$ oz)
eggs	1 or 2
salt	pinch
pepper	shake
milk	1 dessertspoon

to garnish:
parsley	small sprig

These ingredients will make 1 serving.

You will use:

bread knife, bread board, flat-bladed knife, serving plate, basin, fork, saucepan, wooden spoon.

1 Light the gas grill or switch on the electric grill.

2 Toast and butter the bread. Keep warm on a plate in the warming drawer or a very low oven while cooking the eggs.

3 Break the egg or eggs into a basin, add salt, pepper and milk, and beat with a fork.

4 Melt a little butter in a saucepan. Add the egg and milk. Turn heat very low and cook slowly.

Stir with a wooden spoon, moving the
egg from the bottom of the pan all the
time, until the mixture begins to thicken.

Remove pan from heat, for the egg
continues to cook in the hot saucepan.
**Never allow scrambled egg to get
too set.**

Pile on to hot buttered toast, put the
parsley on top. Serve at once.

It is easier to wash the saucepan if you
put it to soak at once in cold water.
One egg makes a small portion
suitable for breakfast. For a more
generous helping, use 2 eggs.

57

Sardines on toast

Canned sardines make good supper dishes and are nice in salads. Ask a grown-up to open the can with the special key.

You will need:

bread	1 slice
butter or margarine	15 grammes ($\frac{1}{2}$ oz)
sardines	2–3
parsley	sprig

These ingredients will make 1 serving.

You will use:

bread knife, bread board, flat-bladed knife, fork, basin (see stage 3), plate.

1 Light the gas grill or switch on the electric grill.

2 Toast the bread on both sides; butter on one side.

3 Either put sardines whole on the toast, or mash them in a basin first, then spread over the toast.

4 Put the toast back under a hot grill for 2 minutes and arrange parsley on top before serving.

Poached haddock

This smoked yellow fish is good for breakfast or supper.

You will need:

smoked haddock	1 medium fillet
water	about ½ litre (1 pint)
butter or margarine	2 small pieces

These ingredients will make 2 servings.

You will use:

kitchen scissors or knife, chopping board, bowl, kitchen paper, measuring jug, large saucepan, fish slice, serving dish.

1 Cut the fish in 2 pieces, wash in cold water, dry on kitchen paper.

2 Put the water and fish into the saucepan and bring the water to the boil; turn down the heat, simmer gently for 5 minutes until the fish is tender.

3 Lift the fish out of the liquid with a fish slice and place on previously warmed dish.

4 Serve with pieces of margarine or butter on top.

Cheese dreams

A quick and delicious supper dish of fried sandwiches. Use ready-sliced bread if possible so the slices are an even thickness.

You will need:

bread	8 slices
butter	75–100 grammes (3–4 oz).
cheese	50–75 grammes (2–3 oz)
fat for frying	50 grammes (2 oz)

These ingredients will make about 4 good servings.

You will use:

flat-bladed knife, bread board for bread and butter, grater, plate, sharp knife, frying-pan, fish slice, serving dish.

1 You will use the gas boiling ring or electric hotplate.

2 Spread the bread with the butter, keep on the board.

3 Grate the cheese on to a plate.

4 Cover half the slices of bread and butter with the grated cheese.

5 Put the rest of the slices of bread and butter over the cheese to make sandwiches.

6 Cut the sandwiches into neat fingers. There is no need to cut off the crusts.

7 Heat the fat in the frying-pan but be very careful it does not become too hot. Fry until the sandwiches are crisp and golden brown on the underside.

8 Turn carefully with a fish slice and fry on the second side.

9 Lift out on to hot serving dish and eat at once.

Grilled bacon and sausages

Perhaps you would prefer to use the grill rather than the frying-pan to cook bacon and sausages. Grilling makes the food less fatty than frying, and is just as quick and easy.

You will need:

sausages	1–2
bacon	1–2 rashers
tomato	1

These ingredients will make 1 serving.

You will use:

fork, sharp knife, chopping board, plate, tongs.

1 Switch on or light the grill.

2 Prick the sausages, put on the grid of grill pan and put under hot grill.

3 Cook for 8–10 minutes, turning, so they brown evenly all over. Add rasher of bacon with the rind cut off and tomato halves, and finish cooking. You will need to turn the bacon once if thick, but there is no need to turn the tomatoes.

4 Serve with mustard if wished. You do not need gravy.

When grilling a lot of bacon and sausages you may not have room for both in the pan, so cook the sausages first, put on a hot dish and keep warm. Then cook the bacon and tomatoes.

Fried bacon and sausages

Fried bacon and sausages make a quick supper dish. If you would rather grill than fry these, see the previous recipe.

You will need:

sausages	1 or 2
bacon	1–2 rashers
mustard for serving	
(optional)	

These ingredients will make 1 serving.

You will use:

fork, frying-pan, plate for keeping sausages warm, serving plate, tongs.

1 Light the gas burner or switch on the electric hot-plate. Put plates to warm in very low oven or warming drawer.

2 As sausages take longer to cook than bacon, these are cooked first.

3 Prick each sausage with a fork to stop the skins splitting.

4 Put into the frying-pan without fat.

5 Cook slowly, turning the sausages as they brown. Large sausages will take about 15 minutes, chipolata sausages will take about 10 minutes.

6 When the sausages are cooked, put them on to a hot plate.

7 Prepare and cook the bacon (see pages 11–12) and serve with the sausages. Most people like mustard with sausages. You can make this up from powder or use made mustard.

Kinds of sausages:
Sausages are usually made from pork, but you can buy beef sausages too. There are many types:

1 Sausages from the butcher or grocer with skins.

2 Sausages without skins. Sometimes these are frozen and you do not need to let them thaw out before you cook them.

3 Smaller sausages that are called chipolata.

4 Frankfurter sausages which you buy in tins or from grocers. These are ready-cooked and just need heating in hot, *but not boiling*, water.

Stuffed jacket potatoes

Potatoes are more interesting and become a more complete meal if you stuff them.

You will need:

old potato	1 large
bacon	1 rasher
tomato	1
salt	pinch
pepper	shake

These ingredients will make 1 serving.

You will use:

scrubbing brush, knife, cloth, fork, chopping board, baking tray, kitchen scissors, frying-pan or saucepan, teaspoon, basin, serving plate.

1 To cook the potato allow approximately 2 hours in a very moderate oven (325°F. 170°C. or Gas Mark 3) *or* 1¼–1½ hours in a moderately hot oven (400°F., 200°C., Gas Mark 6).

2 Scrub potato well, cut out any eyes and dry with a cloth. Prick the potato with a fork to prevent the skin from bursting as the potato cooks.

3 Put on to the oven shelf, or on a baking tray. This makes it easier to take out of the oven. Cook the potato until it feels soft.

4 Remove the rind from the bacon and cut the bacon into tiny pieces; fry for a few minutes, add the tomato, also chopped. Fry for a minute more.

5 Take the cooked potato out of the oven, holding it in a tea-cloth so you do not burn your fingers. Cut a slice off the top, scoop out pulp with a teaspoon, put it into a basin and mash with a fork.

6 Mix with the bacon, the tomato, a pinch of salt and a shake of pepper.

7 Pile the mixture back into the potato case, and heat for 10 minutes in the oven.

Other ways to make jacket potatoes interesting:

Use 25–50 grammes (1–2 oz) grated Cheddar cheese at stage 6 instead of bacon and tomato, and mix this with the mashed potato, salt and pepper. Then continue as stage 7.

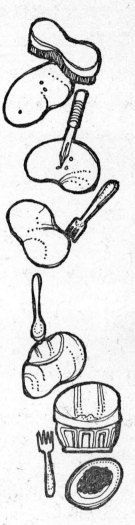

67

Cauliflower cheese

This makes a cauliflower into a complete meal.

You will need:

small cauliflower	1
salt	pinch
water	about ½ litre (1 pint)

for the sauce:

cheese	50–100 grammes (2–4 oz)
flour	25 grammes (1 oz)
salt	pinch
pepper	shake
milk	¼ litre (284 ml) or ½ pint
butter or margarine	15–25 grammes (½–1 oz)

for the topping:

grated cheese	1 tablespoon
breadcrumbs	1 tablespoon

to garnish:

chopped parsley	1 teaspoon

These ingredients will make 3–4 servings.

You will use:

vegetable knife, ovenproof serving dish, measuring jug, saucepan, grater, plate,

basin, wooden spoon, milk saucepan,
colander, tablespoon, teaspoon.

1 Light the gas burner or switch on the
hotplate.

2 Prepare the cauliflower by removing
outside green leaves, and washing
cauliflower thoroughly (leave whole).
Choose an ovenproof serving dish that
just fits the cauliflower and allows it to
stand upright when cooked. It must also
be large enough to take the sauce without
overflowing.

3 Cook cauliflower in boiling salted water
until tender.

4 While it is cooking, prepare the cheese
sauce and topping; warm the serving
dish.

5 To make the sauce, grate the cheese
on to a plate.

6 Mix the flour with salt and pepper in a
basin.

7 Gradually add a quarter of the milk,
stirring with a wooden spoon until you
have a smooth paste.

8 Put the rest of the milk into a saucepan
and bring to boiling point. Take care
it does not boil over.

9 Pour the boiling milk over the flour mixture, stirring all the time to prevent lumps forming.

10 Tip the sauce back into the pan and put over a low heat. Stir until the mixture boils. Then continue boiling for 3 minutes, stirring all the time. Add the butter.

11 When stirring a sauce, make sure that the wooden spoon scrapes across the bottom and into the corners of the pan. If the sauce becomes a little lumpy, remove pan from the heat, beat the sauce with the wooden spoon, or better still with a hand whisk, until it becomes smooth.

12 Add the cheese – do not cook the sauce again.

13 Strain the cauliflower.

14 Put the cauliflower into the serving dish, switch on or light the grill. If you cook and serve this dish quickly, you keep more of the important Vitamin C that is in cauliflower.

15 Pour the cheese sauce carefully over the top of the cauliflower.

16 Sprinkle on the cheese and crumbs; brown for about 3 minutes under the grill.

7 Add chopped parsley and serve at once.

Other ways to use a cheese sauce:

A cheese sauce, made as stages 5 to 12, can be poured over other cooked vegetables; it is especially good over cooked carrots.

You can also make a cheese sauce and serve it with cooked fish fingers.

On pages 72–3 is a recipe for macaroni cheese, which makes a very good dish for dinner or supper.

Macaroni cheese

This is a very filling dish for supper or dinner, and makes a complete meal if you cook a vegetable to have with it or make a salad.

You will need:

water	¾ litre (852 ml) or 1½ pints
macaroni	75 grammes (3 oz)
salt	½ level teaspoon

for the cheese sauce, see pages 68-70.

for the topping:
grated cheese	2 tablespoons
soft breadcrumbs	2 tablespoons
(see page x)	

to garnish:
parsley	few small pieces

These ingredients make 3–4 servings.

You will use:

measuring jug, 2 large saucepans, fork, grater, basin, wooden spoon, sieve, mixing bowl, pie dish.

1 Light the gas burner or switch on the hotplate.

Bring ¾ litre (852 ml) or 1½ pints of water to the boil. Add the salt and put in the macaroni. You may need to break this into convenient-sized pieces. When the water returns to the boil, lower the heat and cook until the macaroni is tender but *not* too soft. Thin macaroni takes approximately 7 minutes, thick macaroni 20 minutes. To test if cooked, press one piece of macaroni against the side of the saucepan with a fork; it will break if cooked.

While the macaroni is cooking, make the cheese sauce as pages 69–70, stages 5 to 12.

Stand a sieve in a mixing bowl and strain the macaroni.

Tip the macaroni into the sauce, mix well, then put into the pie dish.

Sprinkle grated cheese and breadcrumbs over the top.

Either put under the grill for 3–5 minutes to brown or towards the top of a moderately hot oven (400°F., 200°C., or Gas Mark 6) for 15 minutes.

Garnish with small pieces of parsley.

73

Toad-in-the-hole

This is a very good way to turn sausages into a family supper dish.

You will need:

sausages (*large are best*)	4–8
dripping or fat	15 grammes ($\frac{1}{2}$ oz)
for the batter:	
flour (preferably plain)	100 grammes (4 oz)
salt	pinch
egg	1
milk	$\frac{1}{4}$ litre (284 ml) or $\frac{1}{2}$ pint

These ingredients will make 4 servings.

You will use:

sieve, large basin, cup or small basin, wooden spoon, Yorkshire pudding tin, knife, fish slice, serving dish.

1 Sieve the flour and salt into a large basin.

2 Break the egg into a cup or small basin and pour into the flour.

3 Add about $\frac{1}{4}$ of the milk and stir carefully with a wooden spoon until the flour is blended with the egg and milk.

4 Beat really hard until you have a thick smooth mixture. It is now called a thick batter.

5 Some people like to let the thick batter stand before adding the rest of the liquid; others add the liquid straight away. Whichever method you use, pour the rest of the $\frac{1}{4}$ litre (284 ml) or $\frac{1}{2}$ pint of liquid into the thick batter very slowly, beating all the time. When the liquid has nearly all been put in, you may like to change the wooden spoon for a flat whisk. The important thing is to beat well so that the batter does not become lumpy.

6 When all the liquid has been added, let the batter stand in a cool place until you are ready to use it.

7 Set your oven to 425°F. or 220°C. or Gas Mark 7.

8 Grease the bottom of your Yorkshire pudding tin; the picture shows an ideal tin to use for this.

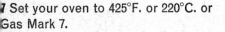

9 Put in the sausages and bake for 10 minutes towards the top of a hot oven.

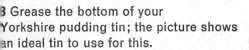
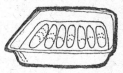

10 Give the batter a final beat if it has been standing; pour it over the sausages.

11 Put back into the hot oven, but this time in the centre of the oven, to make

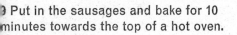

sure the toad-in-the-hole cooks evenly
at the top and bottom. Cook for a further
25–30 minutes, turning the heat down to
moderate after 15 minutes to prevent
burning.

12 Lift out of the tin and serve from the
tin as quickly as possible after cooking.
The batter can take the place of potatoes,
but for a complete dinner serve with
a vegetable such as carrots. For supper,
toad-in-the-hole could be served with
tomatoes or salad.

MAKING SALADS

MAKING SALADS

A good salad depends on the ingredients being fresh. Arrange the ingredients in a bowl or on a flat dish or plate, either in a definite pattern or so that many varied colours are seen. As well as the ingredients below you can use fruit and nuts in salads.

To prepare the usual ingredients for salads:

Lettuce. Wash carefully, pulling the leaves apart. Either dry by shaking in a salad shaker or strain away surplus moisture and put on to a folded tea towel and press gently.

Watercress. Should be washed very carefully in a basin of cold water. Tear off any yellow bits.

Mustard and cress. Use a small amount at a time. Cut away from roots with scissors, hold between finger and thumb and wash. Discard seeds.

Tomatoes. If firm they need not be skinned; just wash and wipe dry. To

emove the skins: put the tomatoes into
basin of boiling water for $\frac{1}{2}$ a minute.
ift out and put into cold water. Take out
f the water and pull away the skin.
lice or halve, or cut into wedges.

ucumber. Leave the skin on if you wish,
r peel thinly with a knife or a potato
eeler. Cut into wafer-thin slices, put on
o a plate or shallow dish, add a little
alt, pepper and vinegar.

adishes. Remove stalk and root from
ase, wash and dry well; slice, if you
vish.

pring onions. Remove outer skin and
oots, cut away surplus green tops, wash
nd dry well.

Raw carrots. These should be scraped if
hey are young, or peeled if old. Rub
gainst a coarse grater.
Cut cooked carrots or other vegetables
nto neat pieces, and add to salads.

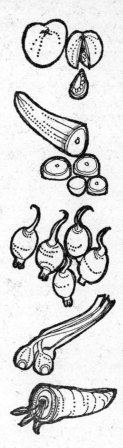

Hard-boiled egg salad

You will need:

eggs	2
lettuce leaves	4–6
tomatoes	2

These ingredients will make 2 servings.

You will use:

saucepan, tablespoon, basin, salad shaker or tea towel, serving plate or dish, chopping board, sharp knife, spoon.

1 Hard-boil the eggs and cool them (see pages 9–10).

2 While the eggs are cooking, prepare the lettuce leaves (see page 78). Arrange on a plate or dish.

3 Cut the tomatoes into slices or quarters, arrange on the lettuce.

4 Cut the shelled eggs into halves or quarters and put on top. Add mayonnaise, if wished.

Cheese salad

You will need:

lettuce leaves	4–6
tomatoes	2
cheese	50–100 grammes
	(2–4 oz)

These ingredients will make 2 servings.

You will use:

salad shaker or tea towel, serving plate or dish, chopping board, sharp knife, grater, large plate.

1 Make the salad base in just the same way as for an egg salad, see page 80.

2 You can put the piece of cheese on the salad, but it looks nicer if you grate it. Stand the grater on a fairly large plate.

3 Pile the grated cheese neatly in the centre of the salad, see picture.

4 If you wish, you can use a hard-boiled egg as well as the cheese, and add mayonnaise.

More cheese salads

Cheese blends very well with fruit, so serve slices of apple, orange or rings of

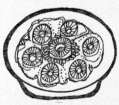

canned pineapple in the salad. Apple
goes a bad colour quickly, so spread a
little mayonnaise or salad dressing over
each slice.
All kinds of cooked vegetables may be
added to a cheese salad; carrots,
potatoes, peas are very good.
Dates, or other dried fruit, and nuts can
be added to cheese in a salad; try cream
cheese or cottage cheese for a change.

Making tomato roses

Only do this if you are used to sharp
knives. Choose a firm tomato and a small
pointed knife.

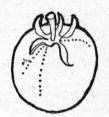

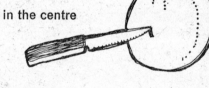

Make a cut downwards in the centre

Now make a second
cut upwards

Continue
like this

Pull the halves apart

Mixed salad

This is the kind of salad you can serve with cold meat or cold fish or cheese.

You will need:

lettuce leaves	4 – 6
tomato	1
cucumber	small piece
hard-boiled egg	1
radishes, etc	a few

To serve:
salad dressing **or**
mayonnaise

These ingredients will make 2 servings.

You will use:

salad shaker or tea towel, chopping board, sharp knife, plate or salad bowl.

1 Prepare the salad ingredients as on pages 78–9.

2 Arrange on a flat plate, in a dish or a salad bowl.

3 Either serve with a salad dressing or mayonnaise.

T–JCB–D

MAKING PUDDINGS

MAKING PUDDINGS

Good puddings and desserts make such
a lot of difference to a meal, and you will
be very popular if you can make them
well.
In many sweets the main ingredient is
fruit. When you cook this take care it is
not overcooked. Test with the tip of a
knife.

To stew fruit – this is cooking fruit
gently in a syrup of sugar and water:

1 Use the same amount of fruit, sugar
and water as the fruit purée opposite.

2 Put the sugar and water into the
saucepan and bring gently to the boil.
This dissolves the sugar. Remove from
heat.

3 Prepare the fruit, and put this into the
sugar and water 'syrup'.

4 Cook gently until tender but still whole.
Hard fruit like apple slices take about
12–15 minutes, soft fruit like blackberries
about 6–8 minutes.

5 The fruit can be served hot or cold
with custard or fresh cream.

Fruit purée

The fruit becomes quite smooth and you can use it with ice-cream or to make the fruit snow (see page 88).

You will need:

*prepared fruit**	200 grammes (8 oz)
water: with soft	
juicy ripe fruit	4 tablespoons
with hard firm fruit	8 tablespoons
sugar	25–40 grammes
	(1–1½ oz)

These ingredients will make 2 servings.

You will use:

tablespoon, saucepan, wooden spoon, sieve, basin.

1 Put the ingredients into a saucepan over a very low heat.

2 Cook, stirring often, until you have a smooth thick mixture.

3 Put a sieve over the basin and rub the fruit through with the wooden spoon if you wish to remove skins or pips.

*This means peeled and sliced apples or halved and stoned plums, or use raspberries, blackberries, gooseberries or other soft fruit.

Fruit snow

This is a very delicious cold dessert
made from fruit purée.

You will need:

fruit purée (see   ⅛ litre (142 ml) **or**
previous page)   ¼ pint
egg white   1

to decorate:
glacé cherries **or**   2
angelica   piece

These ingredients will make 2 servings.

You will use:

2 basins, whisk, tablespoon, glasses or
serving dish, knife.

1 Make the fruit purée (see page 87)
and let it become quite cold.

2 Separate the egg white from the yolk.
You do this by cracking the egg and
allowing the white to drop into one basin
and the yolk into another. Another way
is to break the egg carefully on a plate.
Then put an eggcup over the yolk and
pour the white into a basin.

Stand the basin on a folded tea towel to keep it steady and use an egg whisk to whip the egg white until it is very stiff and stands in peaks when you take the whisk out. The egg yolk is not used in this recipe but could be added to scrambled eggs (see pages 56–7).

Add the white to the fruit purée and fold together. Turn the metal spoon *gently* and *slowly* to mix the egg white and fruit. If you are too rough you lose the light texture.

Put into glasses or a serving dish.

Decorate with small pieces of glacé cherry or angelica.

Fruit salad

There are many ways of making a fruit salad. The easiest is to use canned and fresh fruit together.

You will need:

apricots, pineapple or peaches	1 small can
grapes	a few
orange	1
banana	1
eating apple	1
ripe pear	1

These ingredients will make 3 servings or 4–5 with ice-cream as well.

You will use:

can opener, basin, plate, knife, serving dish.

1 Open the can of fruit, pour the syrup into a basin. Put the fruit on a plate, cut into neat pieces; add to syrup.

2 Halve the grapes, remove the pips. Peel the orange, take out segments of fruit and remove the skin and pips*.

3 Peel banana, apple and pear and cut into neat pieces. Do this just before serving so that they keep a good colour.

4 Mix the fresh fruit with the canned fruit and syrup; put into serving dish.

*This is quite difficult to do. If you find you are breaking the orange segments then just take out the pips and leave the skin, or ask a grown-up to help you.

In summertime you can add other fruit such as cherries, raspberries, etc, to the fruit salad.

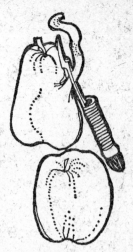

To serve with fruit salad:

You can serve cold custard sauce, made according to the instructions on the custard powder tin. When you have made the custard pour this into a serving bowl or jug.
Cut a circle of greaseproof paper to fit the top of the jug or bowl, make it quite damp and put it over the top of the custard. As the custard cools the damp paper prevents a skin forming. Or you can serve ice-cream with the fruit salad, or fresh cream in a jug.

Fruit jelly

A jelly makes a light pudding. You can put the jelly into 4 dishes at stage 3 if you prefer.

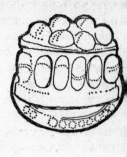

You will need:

water	approx ½ litre (568 ml) or approx 1 pint (see jelly packet)
fruit jelly	½ litre (568 ml) packet or 1 pint packet

These ingredients will make 4 servings.

You will use:

measuring jug, kettle or saucepan, basin to dissolve jelly, tablespoon, another basin or mould, serving plate or dish.

1 Heat the water and dissolve the jelly as instructed on the packet; cool slightly.

2 Rinse out a ½ litre (1 pint) basin or mould with cold water. This helps in turning out the jelly.

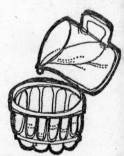

3 Pour the jelly into dishes or mould and leave in a cool place to set. If putting into the refrigerator, make sure the liquid is no longer steaming.

4 To turn out:

(a) Put a serving plate or dish in clean cold water and shake it nearly dry. This will enable you to move the jelly into the right position on the dish without breaking it.

(b) Dip the mould into warm water for 5 seconds to loosen jelly.

(c) Put the plate over the top of the mould. Hold firmly and turn over so that the plate is now under the mould. Shake gently and lift away the mould.

To make jelly more interesting:

1 Add 2 sliced bananas to the cooled jelly at stage 1.

2 Open a small can of mandarin oranges or other fruit, strain off the juice from the can and add enough water to make up to the $\frac{1}{2}$ litre (1 pint) or as given on the packet. Heat and use this at stage 1, then add the fruit to the cooled jelly.

3 Make a milk jelly, as in the following recipe:

Milk jelly

This makes an interesting change from an ordinary fruit jelly and is more nourishing.

You will need:

fruit jelly	½ litre (568 ml) packet or 1 pint packet
hot water	⅛ litre (142 ml) or ¼ pint
milk	approx ⅜ litre (426 ml) or approx ¾ pint

These ingredients will make 4 servings.

You will use:

kettle or saucepan for small quantity of water, measuring jug, basin, tablespoon, mould, serving dish.

1 Dissolve the jelly as instructed on the packet, but use only ⅛ litre (142 ml) or ¼ pint of water.

2 ALLOW TO COOL but not to set, then stir in the cold milk to give ½ litre (568 ml) or 1 pint of jelly liquid.

3 Pour the milk jelly into a mould. Leave to set and turn out.

Ice-cream and hot chocolate sauce

An easy way to make a special sweet with ice-cream.

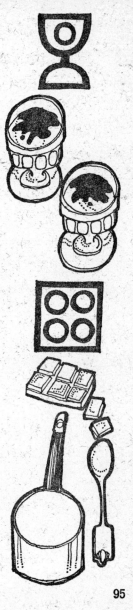

You will need:

ice-cream	2 portions
bar plain chocolate	50 grammes (2 oz)
water	1 tablespoon

These ingredients are for 2 servings.

You will use:

basin, saucepan, tablespoon, 2 serving dishes or sundae glasses.

1 Light the gas burner or switch on the electric hot-plate.

2 Half fill the saucepan with cold water and stand the basin over this.

3 Break the chocolate into small pieces and put into the basin with the water.

4 Put onto the heat and leave until the chocolate has melted.

5 Arrange the ice-cream in glasses.

6 Spoon the chocolate sauce over the ice-cream.

This recipe can very easily be turned into the following party dessert:

95

Chocolate walnut sundae

You will need:

ice-cream, chocolate sauce, a few
walnuts.

You will use for this and the sundae
on page 98:

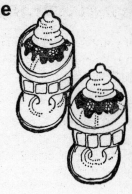

2 or 3 large spoons, sundae glasses, a
chopping board and knife, basins and
forks.

1 Put vanilla, coffee or chocolate ice-
cream into sundae glasses or any
pretty bowls you may have and top with
chocolate sauce made as page 95.

2 Sprinkle over a few chopped nuts or
leave the nuts whole.

Another chocolate sauce

If you have no chocolate you can make a
good sauce with cocoa and other
ingredients.

For 2 people you will need:

margarine	15 grammes ($\frac{1}{2}$ oz)
cocoa	2 level tablespoons
golden syrup	2 level tablespoons
water	2 tablespoons

You will use:

saucepan, tablespoon, wooden spoon.

1 Put all the ingredients for the sauce
into a small pan and heat until the
margarine and cocoa have quite dissolved.

2 *Stir well* all the time and use as the
chocolate sauce (see page 95).

Fruit sundae

You will need:

fresh fruit such as strawberries, raspberries or sliced bananas (kept white by sprinkling with lemon juice) or canned fruit, ice cream, jelly (if ready set), see page 92, some thick cream.

You will use:
utensils as page 96.

1 Put a layer of the fresh or well-drained canned fruit into a sundae glass, top with some ice-cream.

2 Whisk the jelly in a basin with a fork, put on the rest of the ice-cream.

3 Whip the cream in another basin and spoon on to the top of the sundae then decorate with a piece of fruit.

To whip cream:

Choose thick (often called double) cream. Pour it into a basin, then whisk hard with a fork or a hand or rotary whisk until it stands up in peaks.

Baked apple

When you bake an apple in the oven you keep all the flavour of the fruit. Follow the directions in stages 2 and 3 carefully.

You will need:

cooking apples   2 medium or large

This will make 2 servings.

You will use:

apple corer or potato peeler, oven-proof baking dish, sharp knife.

1 The apples can be cooked in a very moderate oven (325°F., 170°C. or Gas Mark 3). Allow 50 minutes–1 hour for small to medium apples, 1–1¼ hours for large apples; or cook for approximately 35–40 minutes for small to medium, 40-50 minutes for medium to large apples in a moderately hot oven (375°–400°F., 190°–200°C., or Gas Mark 5–6).

2 Wash and dry the apples and remove the centre core with an apple corer or potato peeler. Stand in ovenproof baking dish.

3 Slit the skin round centre with the tip of a sharp knife to prevent it bursting in cooking.

Stuffed baked apples

A stuffing makes the apples more interesting. The apples can be filled before baking with any of the following. The amounts are enough for 2 large apples.

1 4 teaspoons dried fruit and 4 teaspoons sugar.

2 4 teaspoons brown sugar topped with 25 grammes (1 oz) butter.

3 2 tablespoons bramble jelly.

4 2 tablespoons golden syrup.

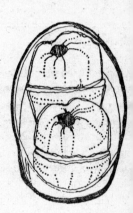

To stuff the apples:

Core as stage 2, put the apples into the baking dish, spoon the filling in the centre holes and cook as stage 1.

Fruit crumble

A nice pudding to eat hot. We have used apples here but you could use plums or other fruit.

You will need:

fruit	200 grammes (8 oz)
water	1–2 tablespoons
sugar	25 grammes (1 oz)

for the crumble:

flour (plain or self-raising)	50 grammes (2 oz)
margarine	25 grammes (1 oz)
sugar	25 grammes (1 oz)

These ingredients will make 2 servings.

You will use:

sharp knife, basin, strainer, small pie dish, plates for sugar, flour, margarine, sieve, mixing bowl, tablespoon.

1 Set your oven to 375°F. or 190°C. or Gas Mark 5.

2 Prepare the fruit; peel apples and cut into thin slices, keep in a basin of cold water until ready to use, to keep as white as possible, then strain away the water.

3 Put the prepared fruit into a small pie dish – about ¼ litre (284 ml) or ½ pint size.

4 Sieve flour into a mixing bowl; some people like to add a pinch of salt.

5 Add the margarine and rub in as described on page xii; add the sugar.

6 Sprinkle the crumble mixture over the fruit; press down with the tips of your fingers; make sure no crumbs of flour, etc, are on the rim of the dish (see picture).

7 Bake in the centre of a moderate oven for 25 minutes. While this pudding is cooking make custard sauce (see page 91) to serve with it, or have cream.

Pink foam apples

This cold dessert is very good for a party. To pour out the evaporated milk, make 2 holes in the can with a can opener or open the can in the usual way.

You will need:

topping:
evaporated milk	1 small can
rose hip syrup	2 tablespoons

large sweet apples	2
lemon juice	1 tablespoon
seedless raisins	2 tablespoons
rose hip syrup	2 tablespoons

These ingredients will make 4 servings.

You will use:

can opener, large basin, whisk, tablespoon, small sharp knife, large plate, lemon squeezer, 4 dishes.

1 Make the topping: pour the evaporated milk into a basin, whisk until it is like thick cream. You will find this quite hard work, so stop during whisking for a few minutes if your arm aches.

2 Stir in the first 2 tablespoons of rose hip syrup.

103

3 Peel, quarter and core the apples and slice them very thinly on to the plate.

4 Pour over the lemon juice, then turn apple slices over.

5 Arrange the apple slices in the four dishes, top with raisins.

6 Spoon over the rest of the rose hip syrup, allow to stand for a few minutes.

7 Spoon over the topping.

Another cold dessert made like this:
You can use fresh pears instead of apples and you could use fresh thick cream instead of evaporated milk.

No-bake blackberry betty

This makes a very good autumn pudding.

You will need:

cooking apples	200 grammes (8 oz)
blackberries	200 grammes (8 oz)
sugar	50 grammes (2 oz)
water	1 tablespoon

crumb mixture:

butter	50 grammes (2 oz)
fresh white breadcrumbs*	150 grammes (6 oz)
soft brown or Demerara sugar	50 grammes (2 oz)

to decorate:

uncooked ripe blackberries	a few

These ingredients will make 6 servings.

You will use:

sharp knife, 2 saucepans, wooden spoon, tablespoon, glasses or glass dish.

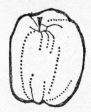

1 Light the gas burner or switch on the hotplate.

2 Peel and slice the apples.

*To make crumbs (see page x).

3 Gently stew the apples, blackberries and sugar together with 1 tablespoon water until the fruit is tender, stir once or twice.

4 Melt the butter in another saucepan. Remove from the heat and mix in the crumbs and sugar; mix with the spoon.

5 Fill glasses or a glass dish with alternate layers of fruit and crumb mixture, finishing with a layer of crumb mixture.

6 Leave to stand for a few hours, preferably overnight.

7 Decorate with raw blackberries, serve by itself or with cream, ice-cream or custard.

Fruit is tender when it feels soft if tested with the tip of a knife.

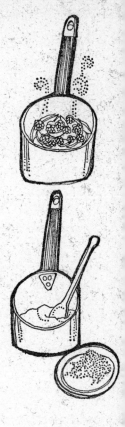

Baked bananas

A new way of cooking bananas.

You will need:

bananas	2 large or 4 small
butter or margarine	25 grammes (1 oz)
brown sugar	2 tablespoons

These ingredients are for 2 servings.

You will use:

plates for bananas, sugar and butter, ovenproof dish, flat knife, tablespoon, serving dishes.

1 Set your oven to 375°–400°F. or 190°–200°C. or Gas Mark 5–6.

2 Peel the bananas and put these into an ovenproof dish.

3 Spread the butter over the fruit and sprinkle with the sugar. This makes a sauce.

4 Bake for 20 minutes in a moderately hot oven.

5 Serve with cream, ice-cream or custard.

Orange baked bananas

You may now make a more interesting
pudding by adding orange juice.

You will need:

Ingredients as baked bananas plus 1
large orange.

1 Squeeze the juice from the orange.

2 Prepare the oven and bananas as
stages 1 and 2 opposite.

3 Spread the butter over the fruit and
sprinkle with the sugar, then add orange
juice.

4 Cook and serve as stages 4 and 5
on page 107.

TEA TIME

TEA TIME

It is very pleasant and not too difficult to prepare the food for tea. Here are some of the things that go to make up a really good tea.

Sandwiches. The recipes are on pages 38–44; cut these smaller for tea than for a picnic or supper snack.

Scones. Either buy these or make them. Serve with butter and jam. You will find the recipe for scones on pages 113–17. Or cut slices of bread and butter and serve with jam.

Cakes. There are many recipes from pages 124–30.

Tea. Served with milk and sugar; younger children may like milk or lemonade.

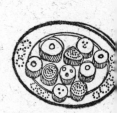

If you are planning a 'high-tea', you can include a more substantial dish, either some kind of salad, see pages 78 to 83, or savoury, see pages 46 to 76.

.aying the table for tea

Put a cloth on the table, lay a small
late and knife for each person, with a
erviette.

Add cups and saucers, teaspoons, a
ug of cold milk, the sugar basin and a
at or stand for the teapot.

Arrange the sandwiches on a plate;
nake these look pretty with parsley or
vashed lettuce leaves.

Either cut the scones across the
niddle and spread with butter and jam
r serve them whole on a plate with
utter in a dish (you will need a butter
nife) and jam in a dish with a spoon.

If you are serving bread and butter
ut this CAREFULLY. Cut the loaf
lownwards on the bread board with a
read knife so you cannot cut yourself.
Spread the bread with butter. You need a
ounded knife not a sharp knife for this.

Arrange the slices or halved slices
eatly on a plate.

Put the cakes on a plate; some people
ike to use a doily.

If you are having a 'high tea', you
vill need large knives and forks and
eat-resistant mats under the plates
f the food is hot.

111

9 Make the tea and carry this in carefully. You can also have a spare jug of boiling water to fill up the teapot. Stand this on a mat.

Tea on a Tray
Many people do not like a 'sit-down' tea.

Arrange the cups and saucers on a tray with the teaspoons, jug of milk and sugar basin. You can cover the tray with a traycloth if you wish.

Carry in the small plates, knives (if needed) and serviettes, also the plates of food.

Do NOT attempt to put the teapot on the tray; carry in the tray, *then* the teapot, *then* the hot water.

ALWAYS put teapots and jugs of very hot water in a safe place away from small children.

Making scones

Here is an easy recipe for home-made scones. These are very good to eat when fresh; if they have become stale you can cut them through the centre, then toast the two halves and spread them with butter or margarine.

Here are some of the ways to make sure your home-made scones are successful:

Make sure the oven is really hot before the scones are put in to cook.

Try to make the scones as quickly as possible and do not handle the mixture more than you need.

Plain scones

You will need:

self-raising flour or (*plain flour and 1 level teaspoon baking powder*)	100 grammes (4 oz)
salt	pinch
margarine or butter	15–25 grammes (½–1 oz)
milk	approx 4 tablespoons

These ingredients will make 4 scones.

You will use:

mixing bowl, sieve, wooden spoon, tablespoon, palette knife, flour sifter, pastry board, rolling pin, baking tray, wire cooling tray, serving plate.

1 Set your oven to 425°F. or 220°C. or Gas Mark 7.

2 Place the bowl on the table, put the sieve over this, then push either the self-raising flour and salt, *or* plain flour, salt and baking powder through the sieve into the bowl; use the wooden spoon.

3 Rub the fat into the flour with the tips of your fingers (see page xii)

4 Add 2 tablespoons of milk, mix with the flour and fat, using a palette knife.

dd another tablespoon of milk and
mix again. You will find that the dough
is beginning to come together. For this
quantity of flour you will need
approximately 4 tablespoons of milk, but
add the fourth tablespoon very slowly so
that you do not put in too much.

The dough is ready when it will form a
ball and leave your mixing bowl clean.

Put down the palette knife and use the
tips of your fingers to gather the dough
together.

Shake a little flour from the flour sifter
or flour dredger onto your pastry board
and shake a small amount of flour over
the rolling pin.

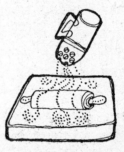

Roll out the scone dough gently and
firmly into a thick round, as shown in
picture. If the edges of the round get
untidy, just neaten them with your hands.

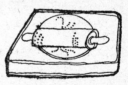

When you have a neat round, mark this
into 4 sections.

0 This is ready to go on to the baking
sheet or baking tray. A plain scone like
this could be baked on an ungreased
baking tray, but some people prefer
greasing the tray. Put the scone on the
tray – it is then ready to be baked.

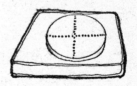

11 A whole scone round, as this is called, should be baked just above the middle of the oven.

12 If you separate the 4 sections into triangles, see picture, you could bake these towards the top of the oven as they cook more quickly.

13 Bake scone round for approximately 15–20 minutes towards the top of a hot oven.

14 Lift from the baking sheet or tray onto a wire cooling tray.

15 Serve scones hot or cold, with butter and jam.

Note!
You can also cut the scones into small rounds with a pastry cutter, after you have rolled out the dough at stage 7. These round scones should be baked on a tray near the *top* of the oven for 10–12 minutes.

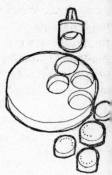

Other kinds of scones

A sweet scone
Add 1 tablespoon of sugar to the flour and fat mixture at stage 3, or instead of sugar use 1 tablespoon honey or golden syrup or black treacle; you will then need less milk, and will need to grease the baking tray (see page xi).

Fruit scones
Add 1 tablespoon of sugar and 1 tablespoon or 25 grammes (1 oz) dried fruit – currants, sultanas, mixed fruit – to the rubbed-in mixture at stage 3.

Cheese scones
Sieve $\frac{1}{4}$-level teaspoon salt, a shake of pepper and a pinch of dry mustard with the flour at stage 2. Rub in the margarine, then add 25 grammes (1 oz) finely grated cheese, then mix with the milk. You will need to grease the baking tray (see page xi).

Rock buns

Simple-to-make buns for tea. They are crisp and sweet and extra nice if you eat them when fresh.

You will need:

self-raising flour	100 grammes (4 oz)
margarine	50 grammes (2 oz)
castor sugar	50 grammes (2 oz)
egg – very small	1
dried fruit	50 grammes (2 oz)
to give a shiny top:	
sugar	1–2 teaspoons

These ingredients will make about 5–6 buns; if using the metric measurements you have a smaller quantity.

You will use:

baking tray, pastry brush, sieve, mixing bowl, basin, fork, palette knife, 2 teaspoons, saucers or plates for sugar and dried fruit, wire cooling tray, serving plate.

1 Set your oven to 400°–425°F. or 200°–220°C or Gas Mark 6–7, page xiv tells you all about ovens.

2 Grease a baking tray; page xi tells you how to do this.

Sieve the flour into a mixing bowl, so there are no lumps. If you find only plain flour in the cupboard, then sieve 1 LEVEL teaspoon baking powder with the flour so your cakes rise well.

Rub in the margarine, you do this with the tips of your fingers; the sketch shows how this is done.

Add the sugar and dried fruit.

Break the egg into the basin and beat the egg with a fork. Add to the rest of the ingredients in the mixing bowl; if it was a large egg, then do not use it all. Add it slowly.

Mix with the knife until the cake dough stands up in points, see the picture.

If you have any egg left, put it into a small cup and cover with 1 tablespoon cold water; later you can add it to scrambled eggs.

Put 5–6 equal-sized 'heaps' on to the baking tray allowing space for them to spread. Use 2 teaspoonsful for this.

10 Sprinkle lightly with a little sugar.

11 Bake towards the top of a moderately hot to hot oven for 10–15 minutes.

12 The cakes are cooked when they are light golden brown in colour and when they feel quite firm as you touch the sides.

13 Lift very carefully with the palette knife on to the wire cooling tray.
If you cannot find a tray like this, then use the grid from the grill pan of your cooker.

Other cakes that are like Rock buns.

Now you have made Rock buns successfully you can make some more cakes like them as I suggest in the following three recipes.

Lemon buns

1 Grate the yellow part of the rind from the lemon on to a plate. The picture shows you how this is done.

2 Add this to the flour in the recipe for Rock buns; as you see, a brush is the best thing to take the rind from the grater.

3 Make the buns just like Rock buns.

Jam buns

1 You use the same mixture as for Rock buns but you do not use dried fruit.

2 Instead you use 1 tablespoon jam.

3 As well you need an extra teaspoon flour.

4 Put a teaspoon of flour on a plate.

5 Make the cake mixture as for Rock buns (see pages 118-20), but do not use quite as much egg, so you can take small pieces of the dough and roll it into balls with your fingers, as in the picture.

6 Put on the greased baking tray, just as Rock buns.

7 Dip your finger in the flour, then press into the centre of each bun to make a hollow.

8 Put a little jam into this, using two teaspoons, then pull the edges of the cake mixture over the jam.

9 Sprinkle with sugar if desired, and bake as before.

Coconut rock buns

Use the same ingredients as Rock buns,
plus 2 level tablespoons desiccated
coconut, which you add at stage 5.

Funny face cakes

Special cakes for a party. Choose
luxury margarine that creams quickly.

You will need:

self-raising flour	100 grammes (4 oz)
castor sugar	100 grammes (4 oz)
easy creaming margarine	100 grammes (4 oz)
eggs	2

for soft glacé icing:
sieved icing sugar	250 grammes (10 oz)
lemon juice	about 3 tablespoons

to decorate:
'*Smarties*' or '*polka dots*', *angelica, currants, chocolate vermicelli*

These ingredients will make about 24 cakes; if using the metric measurements you have a smaller quantity.

You will use:

mixing bowl, sieve, wooden spoon,
teaspoon, paper cake cases, patty tins,
wire cooling tray, basin, tablespoon,
serving plate.

Set your oven to 400°F. or 200°C. or Gas Mark 6.

2 Sieve dry ingredients into a bowl. Add the other ingredients and beat together or 2 minutes until well mixed.

3 Spoon this mixture into about 24 cake cases, arranged in patty tins to keep their shape.

4 Bake above the centre of a moderately hot oven for about 15 minutes. Allow to cool.

5 Sieve the icing sugar and add the lemon juice by degrees, stirring well, until you have a thick icing. Spoon over the cakes.

6 Decorate the cakes with the 'polka dots': currants, etc, to make faces, as shown in the picture.

Chinese chews

These fruit cakes are excellent for a special picnic or party. Chop the dates and nuts carefully or ask a grown-up to do these.

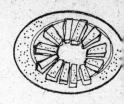

You will need:

margarine or butter	25 grammes (1 oz)
castor sugar	75 grammes (3 oz)
egg	1
vanilla essence	½ teaspoon
self-raising flour	50 grammes (2 oz)
dates	75 grammes (3 oz)
walnuts	25–50 grammes (1–2 oz)

to decorate:
icing sugar	25 grammes (1 oz)

These ingredients will make 12 small fingers.

You will use:

sandwich tin, mixing bowl, wooden spoon, small basin, fork, teaspoon, 3 plates for flour, dates and walnuts, tablespoon, sieve, chopping board, sharp knife, palette knife, small sieve or strainer for icing sugar, serving plate.

1 Set your oven to 375°F. or 190°C. or Gas Mark 4–5. Grease a 20-cm. (8 inch) sandwich tin as page xi and sprinkle with a little flour.

2 Cream the margarine and sugar as page xii.

3 Break the egg into a basin.

4 Measure the vanilla essence carefully, add to the egg, beat with a fork.

5 Gradually beat into the margarine and sugar.

6 Spoon the flour into a sieve and shake into the margarine mixture.

7 Chop the dates and nuts and add to the flour, etc.

8 Spread into the tin and bake for approximately 15 minutes above the centre of a moderate oven.

9 Cool in the tin, then cut into small fingers and coat in icing sugar, and lift out.

10 The easiest way to coat the fingers is to rub the icing sugar through a small strainer or sieve.

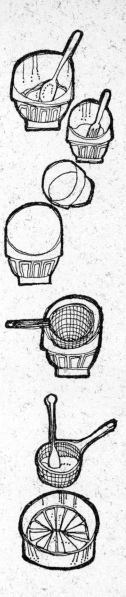

Peach and lemon squares

These can be served for tea or as a new kind of pudding.

You will need:

crumb crust:
butter	75 grammes (3 oz)
digestive biscuits	150 grammes (6 oz)
castor sugar	50 grammes (2 oz)
cinnamon	good pinch

for the filling:
peach slices	1 large can
lemon	1

to decorate:
sliced fresh lemon or	1
crystallized lemon	
slices	12

These ingredients will make 12 squares.

You will use:

basin, wooden spoon, rolling pin, 2 sheets greaseproof paper, baking tin (see stage 4), can opener, strainer, basin, 1 tablespoon, 3 plates, sharp knife, fork, grater, 1 teaspoon, serving dish.

1 Set your oven to 350°F. or 180°C. or Gas Mark 3–4.

2 Cream the butter with the wooden spoon until it is soft.

3 Crush biscuits to fine crumbs between two sheets of greaseproof paper.

4 Stir into the butter with the sugar and cinnamon and press just over half into a 30 cm × 20 cm (12 inch × 8 inch) tin, grease as page xi.

5 Drain the juice from the canned peaches into a basin and lift out the peach slices.

6 Reserve 12 slices for decoration and chop the remainder with a knife and fork.

7 Finely grate the lemon rind.

8 Halve the lemon, take out the lemon pulp with a spoon and chop this with the knife and fork.

9 Mix the chopped lemon and grated rind into the chopped peaches on the plate.

10 Spread this mixture over the crumb crust base.

11 Sprinkle with the remaining crumb crust mixture.

12 Press down lightly with the tips of your fingers.

13 Bake for 35–40 minutes in the centre of a very moderate oven, then chill in the tin.

14 Cut into 12 squares, decorate each square with a peach slice and ½ a lemon or a crystallized lemon slice.

15 Serve cold with ice-cream and the juice from the peaches.

Variations:

Use apricots instead of peaches.

Use cooked, well-drained, apple slices.

Vanilla biscuits

You will need:

self-raising flour	100 grammes (4 oz)
margarine or butter	50 grammes (2 oz)
sugar	50 grammes (2 oz)
vanilla essence	few drops
milk	1–2 teaspoons

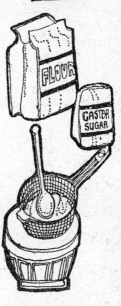

to sprinkle over biscuits:
sugar   1 teaspoon

*These ingredients will make 10–12 biscuits;
if using the metric measurements you
have a smaller quantity.*

You will use:

plates or saucers for the flour,
margarine and sugar, sieve, mixing bowl,
palette knife, skewer, cup, teaspoon,
pastry board, sharp knife, 2 baking trays,
fork, wire cooling tray, serving plate.

1 Set your oven to 350°–375° F. or 180°–
190°C. or Gas Mark 4–5.

2 Sieve the flour into a mixing bowl.

3 Rub in the margarine with the forefinger
and thumb of each hand until it is like
crumbs; or use your fingertips. Add the
sugar.

131

4 To take a few drops of essence from the bottle dip the skewer into this, take it out, let the drops fall into a cup; add 1 teaspoon milk.

5 Pour the milk and vanilla into the biscuit mixture.

6 Knead the mixture very hard with your fingers; page xii tells you about kneading.

7 The mixture should form one ball. If too dry, add another teaspoon of milk. This should be enough.

8 Put on to the pastry board and divide into about 10–12 equal-sized pieces.

9 Roll pieces into neat balls.

10 Place on 2 ungreased baking trays with plenty of room for them to spread out.

11 Flatten slightly with the back of the fork or your hand.

12 Sprinkle the sugar over the biscuits.

13 Bake in a moderate oven, near the centre, for about 15 minutes until golden.

14 Lift out of the oven, cool for 5 minutes on tins so that the biscuits do not break, then lift with a palette knife and place on a wire cooling tray.

15 When quite cold, store in an airtight tin away from bread, pastry or cakes.

Chocolate biscuits

1 Weigh out the flour as for vanilla biscuits, take away 1 level tablespoon flour, put this back in the bag.

2 Add 1 level tablespoon cocoa to the flour.

3 Sieve the flour and cocoa as stage 2 in the vanilla biscuits; continue as for the vanilla biscuit recipe.

PARTIES AND PICNICS

PARTIES AND PICNICS

There are plenty of recipes in this book which you can use when you give a party. Try to plan dishes that can be made well in advance. Each recipe in this book tells you how many people it serves so you will know just how much food to prepare – allow about 3–4 sandwiches for each person.

MENU 1

Here is a menu that is ideal for a buffet-type meal where everyone helps themselves, and is suitable for tea or evening time.

Mixed and open sandwiches (pages 38–44)
Peach and lemon squares (page 128–30)
Fruit salad (page 90–91), with ice-cream
Fruit cup (page 33–4)

Preparations:
1 Make the peach and lemon squares earlier in the day **or** the day before the party; keep in a cool place.

2 Make the fruit salad. Keep the dish covered.

3 Make the fruit cup.

4 Prepare the sandwiches, arrange on plates and cover these with foil or greaseproof paper, or a barely damp, clean teacloth, so that they do not dry. The refrigerator is an ideal storage place.

5 Arrange the food and drink on the table with plates, glasses and serviettes. You will need spoons for the fruit salad.

MENU 2

Here is another good buffet menu, best for small numbers because you must toast the sandwiches just before you eat them, and this would be rather hectic for a lot of servings.

Hot toasted cheese club sandwiches (pages 43–4)
Ice-cream
Coffee (pages 23–4)

Preparations:
1 Arrange the table, make the coffee, put out plates and spoons for the ice-cream.

2 Have the bread and filling ready so that all you have to do at the last minute is the toasting.

MENU 3 – for a WINTER PARTY

It is fun to have some really hot food for a party in wintertime. You could choose a menu similar to menu 1, and open tins of soup to heat and serve hot. If you prefer to make some hot dishes here are two very easy menus.

Stuffed jacket potatoes (pages 66–67)
Hot sausages, grilled or fried (pages 62–5)
Fruit jellies (pages 92-3) with cream
Rolls, butter, and cheese
Coffee and fruit drinks

Preparations:
1 Make the jellies in the morning or the day before so they set.

2 Prepare the jacket potatoes and cook them completely if you wish so they are just ready to heat, or get everything prepared, ie, bacon, etc, cooked so the last-minute preparations are soon made.

3 Cook the sausages by grilling or frying. You can also cook them in a greased tin in the oven when they take about 30–35 minutes.

4 Arrange the table, make the coffee and fruit drinks.

Here are two recipes for
SUMMER PARTIES AND PICNICS, when most of us enjoy cool refreshing food:

MENU 4

Cheese salad and egg salad (pages 81–2 and 80)
Rolls and butter
Pink foam apples (pages 103–4) and vanilla biscuits (pages 131–2)
Cold milk, fruit drink

Preparations:
1 Make the vanilla biscuits several days before the party if wished and keep in an airtight tin.

2 Make the pink foam apples; allow plenty of time for this as it is quite a slow recipe.

3 Prepare the salads on plates or dishes and cover with foil, or kitchen or greaseproof paper so they do not dry.

4 Put out the cold drinks, etc, and lay the table.

138

MENU 5

Cold sausages with hard-boiled eggs (pages 9–10), tomatoes, lettuce
Cheese scones (page 117) and butter
Chinese chews (pages 126–7) and fresh fruit
Lemonade (pages 31–2)

Preparations:

Make the Chinese chews earlier in the day or even the day before; keep in an airtight tin.

Make the cheese scones the day of the party so they are fresh.

Make the lemonade.

Cook the sausages and eggs and shell the eggs; prepare the lettuce.

Arrange the food on plates and trays and take into the garden.

If you wish to use this menu for a picnic then:

Carry the Chinese chews in a tin so they do not break.

Split the scones, spread with butter and then wrap them or put in a tin.

Pour the cold lemonade into a vacuum flask.

Cook the sausages and eggs, shell the eggs, wrap in foil or greaseproof paper or put into plastic picnic boxes.

139

5 Put the washed and dried lettuce into a plastic bag or box or wrap in foil.

When you go on a picnic do remember to bring back all your bags so the place is left tidy.
In case you go looking for blackberries there is a special recipe which I thought you would like on pages 105–6.

Sometimes when you come back from a picnic you may want to make a very quick meal; you could have one of the toasted snacks (pages 43–4) and baked bananas for a pudding, which are on pages 107–8.

If you have enjoyed this
PICCOLO Book, you may like
to choose your next book
from the new PICCOLO titles
listed on the following pages.

Where danger makes exciting history . . .

Piccolo
TRUE ADVENTURES

A magnificent new series for boys and girls from eight to twelve

Full colour covers

Daring deeds

Vivid illustrations

Thrilling true stories

PIRATES AND BUCCANEERS
GREAT SEA MYSTERIES
HIGHWAYMEN AND OUTLAWS
HAUNTED HOUSES
GREAT AIR BATTLES
SUBMARINES

Piccolo
TRUE ADVENTURES 20p EACH

More gripping than any fiction

. . . five, six, seven, eight – What do you appreciate

Piccolo
COLOUR BOOKS

Great new titles for boys and girls from eight to twelve

Fascinating full-colour pictures on every page

Intriguing, authentic easy-to-read facts

DINOSAURS

SECRETS OF THE PAST

SCIENCE AND US

INSIDE THE EARTH

EXPLORING OTHER WORLDS

STORMS

SNAKES AND OTHER REPTILES

AIRBORNE ANIMALS

Piccolo
COLOUR BOOKS 25p EACH

Fit your pocket – Suit your purse

The best in fun – for everyone ...

Piccolo

GAMES AND PUZZLES

101 BEST CARD GAMES FOR CHILDREN

NUT CRACKERS
Puzzles and Games to boggle the mind

FUN AND GAMES OUTDOORS

JUNIOR PUZZLE BOOKS

JUNIOR CROSSWORD BOOKS
The most popular children's crosswords in Britain

BRAIN BOOSTERS

CODES AND SECRET WRITING

Piccolo – Pick of the Puzzles 20p each

Piccolo

SUPERB STORIES – POPULAR AUTHORS

FOLLYFOOT
Monica Dickens. Based on the Yorkshire
Television series

FOXY
John Montgomery

FOXY AND THE BADGERS
John Montgomery. David comes to Sussex from an orphanage and finds
an unusually appealing new friend ...

THE JUNGLE BOOK
Rudyard Kipling

THE SECOND JUNGLE BOOK
Rudyard Kipling. The magic of Mowgli, child of the forest, whose
adventures made him every other child's hero

TALES FROM THE HOUSE BEHIND
by the author of the world-famous Diary of Anne Frank